Alfred's
Teach Yourself To Play Rock Keyboard

JOE BOUCHARD

Everything you need to know to start playing now!

MW00442019

SOFTWARE

In addition to MP3 demonstration tracks, the companion DVD includes Alfred's exclusive TNT 2 software which allows users to customize the audio tracks in this book for practice. Use it to slow down tracks, isolate and loop parts, and change tempos and keys.

To install, insert the DVD into the disc drive of your computer.

Windows
Double-click on **My Computer,** right-click on the DVD drive icon, and select **Explore.** Double-click on the **TnT2** installer file.

Macintosh
Double-click on the DVD icon on your desktop**.** Double-click on the **TnT2.pkg** installer file.

TNT 2 SYSTEM REQUIREMENTS

Windows
XP, Vista, 7, 8
QuickTime 7.6.7 or higher
1.8 GHz processor or faster
1.6 GB hard drive space
2 GB RAM minimum
DVD drive for installation
Speakers or headphones
Internet access for updates

Macintosh
OS 10.4 and higher (Intel only)
QuickTime 7.6.7 or higher
1.6 GB hard drive space
2 GB RAM minimum
DVD drive for installation
Speakers or headphones
Internet access for updates

Alfred Music
P.O. Box 10003
Van Nuys, CA 91410-0003
alfred.com

ISBN-10: 1-4706-1424-3 (Book & DVD-ROM)
ISBN-13: 978-1-4706-1424-9 (Book & DVD-ROM)

Music arranged and performed by Joe Bouchard • Audio recording by Joe Bouchard

CONTENTS

INTRODUCTION

From the honky-tonk piano in the early days of rock and roll to the soulful sounds of the electric organ in the late 1950s and '60s to the advanced synthesizer sounds of the '70s, '80s, and beyond, the electronic keyboard has been an essential part of music—especially rock music. It can also be a source of great fun and deep personal satisfaction.

Now you can teach yourself to play rock keyboard. Get the most out of your instrument by learning the layout of the keyboard, the names of the notes, proper technique for both hands, and in almost no time, you could be playing in a rock band.

Attention guitarists, bass players, drummers, and other instrumentalists: This book is for you, too. In order to fully understand music-making today, you must have some basic keyboard knowledge. When you try to understand how harmonies and song arrangements work, seeing the notes played directly in front of you on a keyboard is an invaluable tool. Furthermore, playing chords will help you to see alterations in harmony that can open up a rich harmonic world for your music.

These days, rock keyboard parts can be recorded into a computer or recording workstation using many different non-keyboard instruments, including a guitar or even singing the part into a computer. But, the most efficient way, by far, to play keyboard parts into songs is with an actual keyboard.

Chords are an essential part of rock keyboard playing, so a thorough look at all the essential chords is necessary. Once you learn the basic chords, you will learn inversions of those chords and be on your way.

What kind of keyboard will I need for this book?

This book is written for the piano, but many parts can be played on an organ or electronic keyboard. Feel free to experiment with different keyboard sounds. Learn all the easy songs in various styles included here, and use them to jam until you're ready for the band!

 # WHAT YOU NEED TO TEACH YOURSELF TO PLAY ROCK KEYBOARD

1. This book.

2. A *piano,* or an *electronic keyboard* with a built-in amplifier and speakers.

3. The *companion recording*, which was produced especially for this book. These tracks can be found on the included DVD-ROM as hi-resolution MP3 files.

4. A *computer* with a DVD-ROM drive to install the TNT 2 software player and to download the companion MP3s.

5. A *metronome* to provide you with a solid, steady rhythm from the beginning. A metronome is an adjustable device that helps you learn to play at the proper *tempo* (speed) and in correct rhythm. There are several free, or inexpensive, metronomes available for your computer or smart device—they can really help you perfect your timing.

SITTING AT THE KEYBOARD

To start, it is important to sit correctly at your keyboard. You will play better if you sit up straight with your elbows even with the keyboard. See the photo to the right.

STANDING AT THE KEYBOARD

Some people prefer to stand to play the keyboard, especially when playing smaller electronic keyboards. The height of the keyboard is important—make sure your wrist is close to parallel with the keys and not at a radical angle. The photo to the right shows the proper height and angle.

TUNING YOUR INSTRUMENT

Traditional pianos need to be tuned by a professional on a regular basis, say a few times a year, while most modern electronic keyboards have a tuning device that will easily adjust the pitch of the instrument. It is important for your instrument to be in tune, so let's tune up with Track 1 of the recording. At the beginning of the track, you will hear a pitch for about 20 seconds. This is the standard A440 pitch that piano tuners usually use. Compare the A note above middle C (see page 9) on your keyboard to the standard A440 pitch on the recording. If your piano doesn't match, call a professional tuner. If your electronic keyboard doesn't match, see the owner's manual for instructions on how to make tuning adjustments.

GETTING STARTED # HOW THE FINGERS ARE NUMBERED

We use a number system to represent the fingers of both hands. The *thumb* is 1, *index* finger is 2, *middle* finger is 3, *ring* finger is 4, and *pinky* finger is 5. Many piano music parts will include finger numbers to help make your playing more efficient. (Note to guitar players: Guitar fingerings are slightly different—where 1 is the index finger and so on. If you're a guitarist learning piano, notice the difference in finger numbers.)

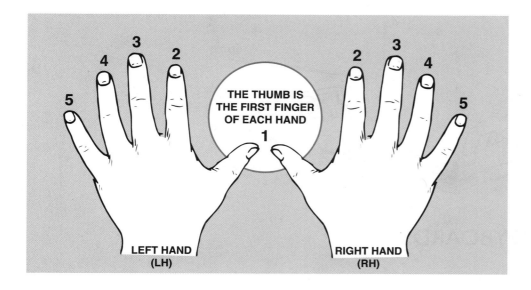

Following is an easy exercise to get in touch with your fingers. To prepare for this exercise, press your hands flatly together with all the fingers touching in a "prayer position." Next, curl your fingers so that only the fingertips are touching.

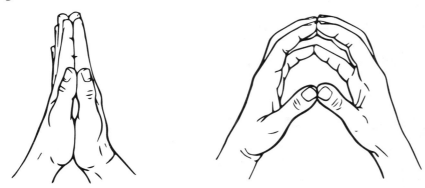

Shake the hands out vigorously, dangling loosely from the wrists, as shown below. Count 1–2–3–4. It's a good idea to keep the fingers loose at first. Use this exercise to shake the tension out of your fingers.

Dangle from wrists   Shake out hands

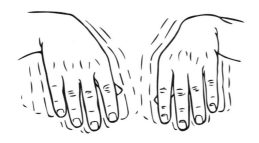

THE MECHANICS OF PIANO KEYBOARDS

The traditional piano keyboard is an amazing invention that has been around since approximately 1700. There were keyboards before, but they were limited in volume—mostly only able to play softly. With the piano, different levels of volume were possible, and composers were thrilled to have this very expressive instrument, literally, at their fingertips!

When you depress a piano key, a hammer inside the piano touches a string to make a tone. When you press into a key with a *little* weight, you make a *soft* tone. When you use *more* weight, you get a *louder* tone.

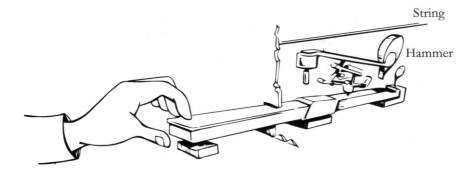

ELECTRONIC KEYBOARDS

Electronic keyboards, like the *electric piano* and *electric organ,* have been popular since the 1950s. In the '60s, *synthesizer keyboards* were developed, leading to all kinds of new sounds. In the '70s, *digital synthesis,* where digital recordings were used to create life-like sounds, became possible. By the '90s, electronic keyboards were able to combine sound samples with synthesis, and hybrid sounds were now possible. Today, amazing new keyboards capable of producing hundreds of quality sounds are available for very reasonable prices.

In the early days, electronic keyboards were only capable of producing one volume—while these keyboards included a volume knob to control the overall output, how hard or soft you pressed the keys did not affect the volume. Organs only had one volume level for each available sound. So, in order to change the volume level, you had to use a different sound or a *volume pedal* on the floor. Today, almost all keyboards are capable of a wide range of expression and are *velocity sensitive,* which means how hard or soft you depress a key will affect its output volume.

DYNAMICS

In order to be a musician you need to understand *dynamics*—loud and soft, and everything in between—and learn about *dynamic signs.* To the right are some common dynamic signs.

pp = *Pianissimo* = Very soft

p = *Piano* = Soft

mf = *Mezzoforte* = Medium loud

f = *Forte* = Loud

ff = *Fortissimo* = Very loud

FOUR REASONS FOR PLAYING WITH CURVED FINGERS

1. When your fingers are straight, each one is a different length. When your fingers are curved, they can be adjusted to be the same length.

2. If your fingers are straight, the thumb cannot be used properly. Curving your fingers will bring the thumb into correct playing position.

 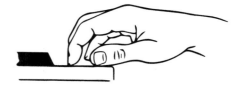

3. Straight fingers will bend at the knuckle, against the motion of depressing the key, delaying key response. With curved fingers, the keys respond instantly, and you are in control!

 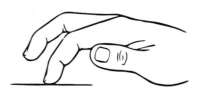

4. To move over the keys, the thumb will need to shift under the fingers and the fingers will, likewise, cross over the thumb. Curved fingers will provide an "arch" shape to make this motion possible.

NOTE: Try to keep your fingernails fairly short. It may be difficult to curve your fingers properly with long fingernails. Plus, playing rock music is hard on the fingertips, so you could break a nail when rocking hard with a band!

If you are sitting at your keyboard for the first time, you are probably asking yourself, "How can I possibly know all the names of this many keys?" It is simple, and it starts with looking carefully at the *black keys*.

THE TWO BLACK-KEY GROUP AND THE THREE BLACK-KEY GROUP

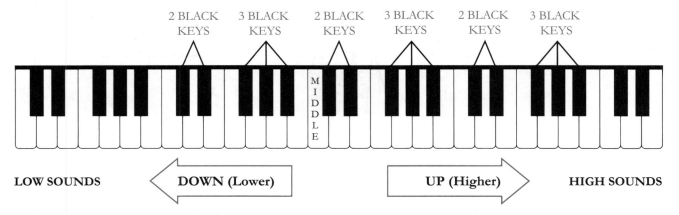

On the keyboard, *down* is to the left, and *up* is to the right. As you move down and left, the tones sound *lower*. As you move to the right and up, the tones sound *higher*.

The piano keys are named with the first seven letters of the alphabet, starting with A.

A B C D E F G

In the image above, notice there is a repeating pattern of black and white keys on the keyboard; the black keys alternate between groups of two and three. We identify each *white key* by its position in between or next to a black-key grouping. For example, the note A is found between the right two black keys of every three black-key group.

The white key marked MIDDLE in the example above is *middle C*. One white key up (to the right) is D. Two white keys up is E and so on. If we start at middle C and go down, to the left, one white key, we find B. Two white keys to the left, and we have A. Learn all the white keys below.

The White Keys in Relation to the Black-Key Groups

 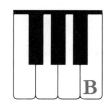  

Now you can name every white key on the keyboard. Remember the notes A, B, C, D, E, F, G are used over and over, and that middle C is closest to the middle of the piano.

The LOWEST key on most pianos is the note A

The C closest to the middle of the piano is called MIDDLE C

GETTING STARTED BEGINNING TO PLAY Track 2

Place your **right hand** on the piano with your **thumb** on middle C as in the diagram below.

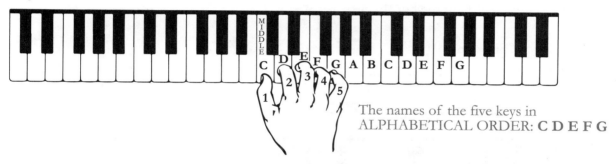

The names of the five keys in ALPHABETICAL ORDER: **C D E F G**

1. Play the notes C, E, G one key at a time with your right-hand fingers, 1, 3, 5. Play moderately loud (**mf**). Remember to keep your fingers curved and relaxed.

2. Move your hand one key to the right, and play D, F, A with your right-hand fingers, 1, 3, 5.

3. Continue to move up the keyboard, shifting your thumb to the next higher white key until you play the next, higher set of the notes you started with: C, E, G.

Next, place your **left hand** on the piano so that your left-hand **finger 5** (pinky) falls on the C below middle C.

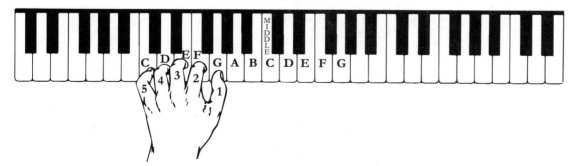

1. Play C, E, G, one key at a time with your left-hand fingers, 5, 3, 1. Play moderately loud (**mf**).

2. Move your hand one key to the right, and play D, F, A with your left-hand fingers, 5, 3, 1.

3. Continue to move up the keyboard, shifting your left-hand finger 5 to a new higher note until you play the next higher set of the notes C, E, G.

RIGHT-HAND C POSITION

Place your right-hand thumb on middle C, and let your right-hand fingers fall naturally on the keys to the right of your thumb. Play these notes—C, D, E, F, G—to get them under your fingers. This is the *right-hand C position.*

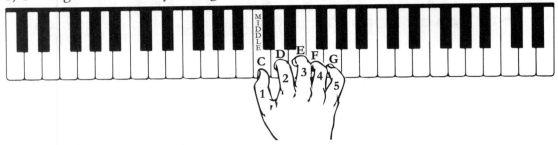

GETTING ACQUAINTED WITH MUSIC

Musical sounds are indicated by round symbols called *notes,* which can be white or black, depending on their value. The name of a note is determined by its location on a graph that consists of five lines and four spaces called a *staff.* We use the *treble staff* to notate the right hand notes in piano music. With the treble clef, you will find middle C on a short line below the staff, called a *ledger line.* The note D is written in the space below the staff. Each next higher note is written on the next higher line or space. Take a look at the diagram below.

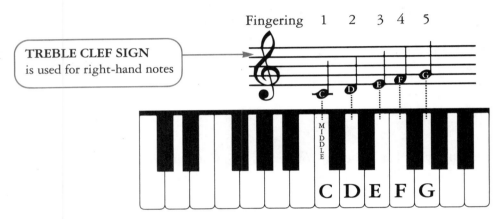

TREBLE CLEF SIGN is used for right-hand notes

QUARTER NOTES Track 3

We measure the duration of notes by how we count them, using a unit of measurement called a *beat* to count. The first type of note we'll learn is the *quarter note,* which gets one beat. Quarter notes are black with a line, called a *stem,* attached to it. Set your metronome to a slow tempo (84 beats per minute, or BPM), and play this exercise while counting each quarter note, 1–2–3–4.

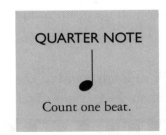

QUARTER NOTE

Count one beat.

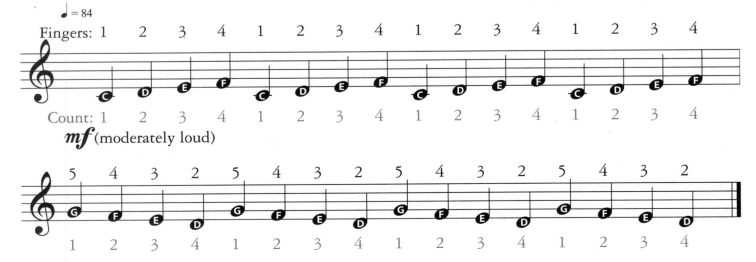

HALF NOTES Track 4

Half notes get two beats and are white with a stem. The exercise features half notes at the end. Remember to keep counting during the half notes, even though on two and four you are not playing anything.

HALF NOTE

Count two beats.

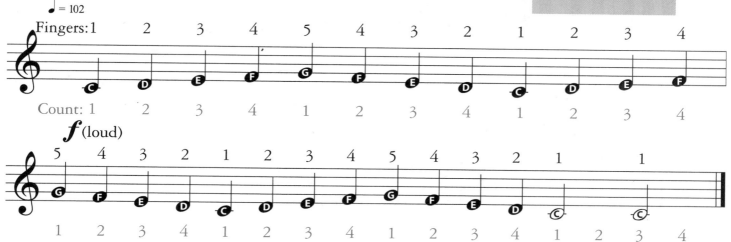

WHOLE NOTES Track 5

The *whole note* gets four beats and is white with no stem. Play the following exercise, which combines quarter notes with whole notes, and features notes that are adjacent (one key apart).

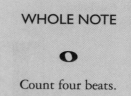

WHOLE NOTE

Count four beats.

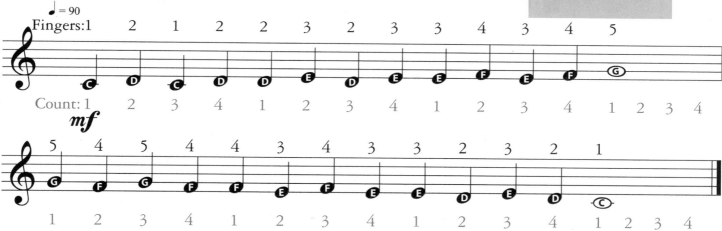

Here's an exercise that incorporates all three note values you've learned. This time, you will be playing notes that skip a key. Remember to keep counting.

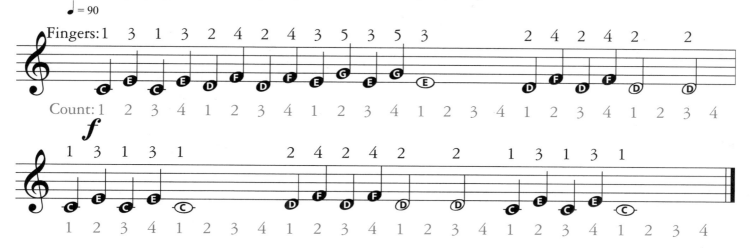

LEFT-HAND C POSITION

Place your left hand on the keyboard so that finger 5 falls on the C below middle C. Let the remaining fingers naturally fall on the white keys to the right of the C note. This is the *left-hand C position.*

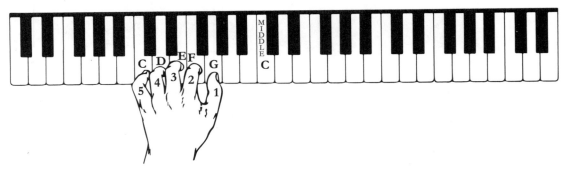

The notes for this position are written on the *bass staff.* Like the treble staff, the bass staff has five lines and four spaces. The note C played by finger 5 in left-hand C position is written on the second space of the bass staff. Each next higher note is written on the next higher line or space.

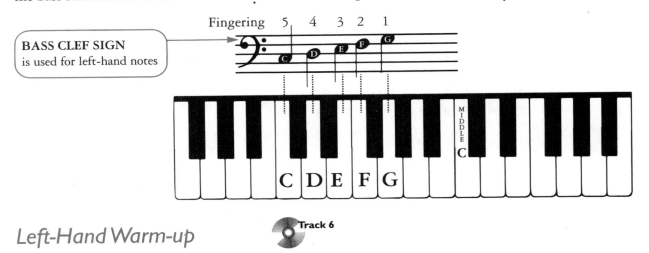

BASS CLEF SIGN is used for left-hand notes

Left-Hand Warm-up

Track 6

The following exercise is written in bass clef and is a great warm-up for your left hand. Begin very slowly and set your metronome to 50 BPM or slower. Try to gradually increase the tempo to 90 BPM.

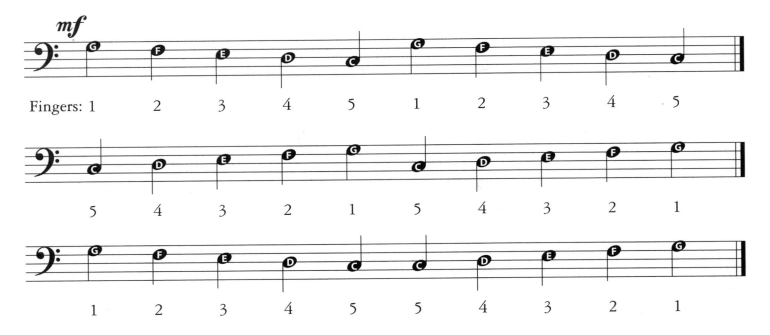

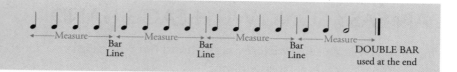

Bar lines divide music into *measures* of equal duration.

$\frac{4}{4}$ TIME

To be musical, it is important to play with a sense of rhythm. We use a sign called a *time signature* at the beginning of a piece of music to indicate the number of beats in each measure. *Four-four time,* or $\frac{4}{4}$, is the most common time signature. It means there are four beats in every measure, and the quarter note gets one beat. Most rock music is in $\frac{4}{4}$ time. Play the following exercises in $\frac{4}{4}$ time, counting 1–2–3–4 as you play.

The following exercise features many repeated notes. Take it slow and steady, and play each note cleanly.

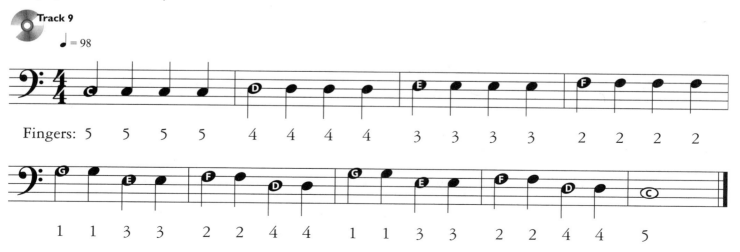

PLAYING AN EASY SONG WITH EACH HAND

Play the following, easy five-note song with the **right hand** only. Remember to count the beats and play this with a steady tempo.

Easy Song for Right Hand

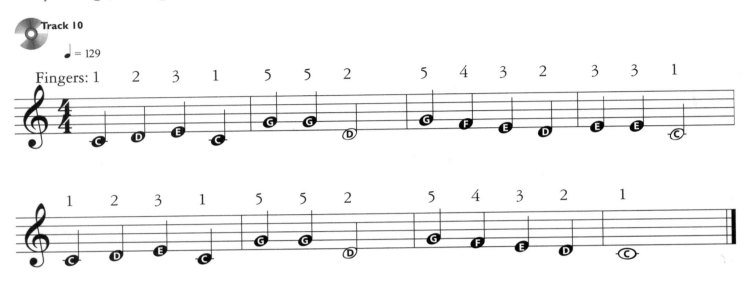

Now, play the easy five-note song with the **left hand** only. Try to match the same steady feeling you had when you played it with the right hand. Notice you are playing the same notes as above but are now using a different hand and reading music in bass clef.

Easy Song for Left Hand

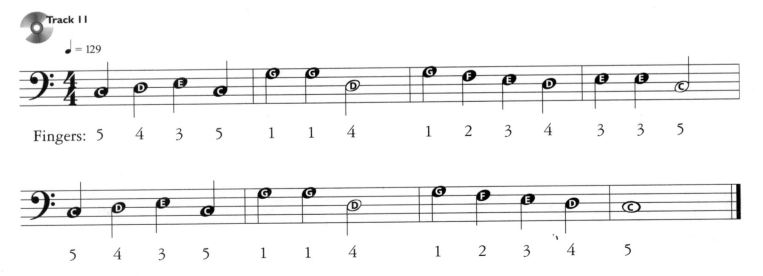

INTRODUCING THE GRAND STAFF

To help with reading music for both the right and left hand, we connect the treble and bass staves with a line and a bracket. This is called the *grand staff*. Check it out below.

Grand Staff

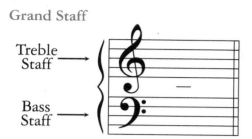

In order for your eyes to see all the notes at once, the eleven lines in the music above are split into two staves—one for the left hand and one for the right. The upper staff is for the right hand and is marked with a *treble clef*. The lower staff is for the left hand and is usually marked with a *bass clef*. The center line of the grid is replaced by a ledger line, which we learned about on page 10.

Now, play "Five-Note Song" with both hands, using the grand staff. Try to sing along if you can!

Five-Note Song

Track 12

♩ = 129

* The fingering numbers are smaller from here through the rest of the book.
  This is a more standard size usually used in piano sheet music.

MELODIC INTERVALS—2NDS AND 3RDS

The musical distance from one note to another is called an *interval.* Intervals have number names such as 2nds, 3rds, etc. Notes played separately make a *melody,* and the intervals between them are called *melodic intervals.* The first melodic interval we will learn is the *2nd,* which, for now, is the distance from any white key to the next white key up or down. 2nds are written line to space or space to line in the music.

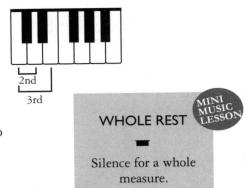

WHOLE REST

MINI MUSIC LESSON

Silence for a whole measure.

Play and sing the following, easy melody which features 2nds.

Track 13

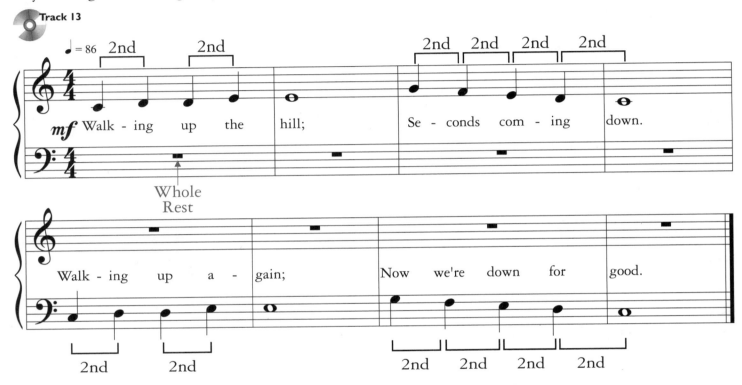

3rds are measured by skipping a white key and going to the next white key either up or down. In the music, 3rds go from line to line or space to space. Play the following melody and look for the 3rds.

Track 14

MELODIC INTERVALS—4THS AND 5THS

When you skip two white keys in a melody, you are playing the melodic interval of a *4th*. An example of a 4th is the distance moving up from a C to an F. 4ths are written line to space, or space to line in the music.

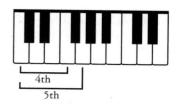

Here's a simple melody that features 4ths.

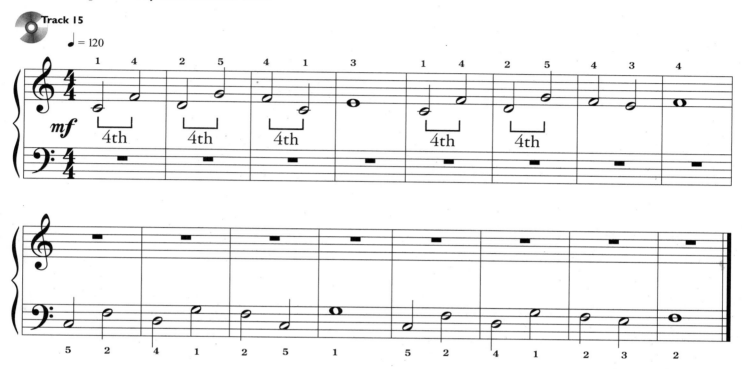

When you skip three white keys in a melody, you are playing a *5th*. 5ths are written line to line, or space to space in the music. Play the example below starting with the left hand.

HARMONIC INTERVALS—2NDS AND 3RDS

Notes played together make *harmony.* We call the intervals between these notes *harmonic intervals.* Play the following exercise using the harmonic intervals of 2nds and 3rds. Note that the distance between keys is the same for melodic and harmonic intervals of the same name. The difference is melodic intervals are notes played in succession, while harmonic intervals are notes played at the same time.

Track 17

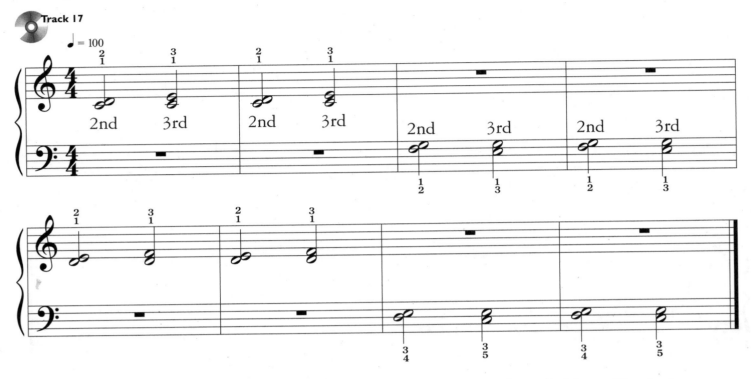

This next piece is based on a melody by the composer Antonín Dvořák. The curved lines between notes are called *phrasing marks.* A *phrase* in music is a connected group of notes that express a complete, independent idea. Playing the phrase-marked notes smoothly and connected is called *legato.* The rhythms are different in each hand, so practice each hand separately first, then combine them.

Going Home

Track 18

HARMONIC INTERVALS—4TH AND 5THS

Following are a couple of pieces that use 4th and 5th harmonic intervals. The harmonic interval of a 5th is also called a *power chord* in rock music and is found in many contemporary rock songs. (We'll learn more about chords on page 22.)

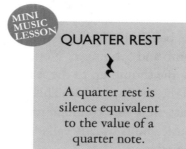

MINI MUSIC LESSON

QUARTER REST

A quarter rest is silence equivalent to the value of a quarter note.

MINI MUSIC LESSON

HALF REST

A half rest is silence equivalent to the value of a half note.

Track 19

Track 20

ROCK RIFFS FOR THE LEFT HAND—
HARMONIC INTERVALS IN 5THS AND 6THS

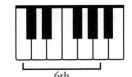

6th

Let's start with a simple rhythm that alternates between the between the harmonic intervals C–G and C–A. C to G is the interval of a *5th*, which we learned earlier skips three white keys. C to A is the interval of a *6th*, which skips four white keys. Practice the example below slowly at first with the thumb and 5th finger. Work on shifting the thumb up to the A note to keep the rhythm steady. This left-hand pattern is very common in early rock music and is usually called a *boogie* figure.

Track 21

♩ = 120

"Rockin' Away" features the boogie figure.

Rockin' Away   Track 22

♩ = 113

This next song uses 5th and 6th harmonic intervals in both hands, along with other intervals we've covered. In the right hand, stretch your 5th finger up to play the 6th interval. Keep both hands steady with a strong beat.

Road to Rock Mountain Track 23

C MAJOR AND F MAJOR CHORDS

A *chord* is three or more notes played together.

The *major chord* is a basic element of harmony and very important to rock piano.

Since it is easy to play three notes with one hand on the keyboard, let's learn several chords that can fill out songs with full-sounding chords. We'll learn the *C Major chord,* which consists of the notes C, E, and G, and the *F Major chord,* consisting of F, A, and C.

Below is a C Major chord for the right hand:

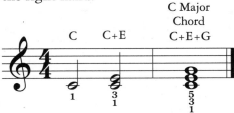

Here is a C Major chord for the left hand:

Here is an F Major chord for the right hand:

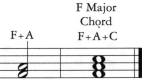

Here is a F Major chord for the left hand:

Below is an F Major chord for the right hand with the notes rearranged to keep your thumb on middle C.

It is common for a chord to **not** have the *root,* or its main letter name, as the lowest note. In these instances, the chord names will be written with a slash followed by a letter that indicates the lowest note. So, F/C indicates an F Major chord with the note C as the lowest note.

These types of chords are called *slash chords* or *inversions.* (We'll learn more about inversions on page 61.)

> **NOTE:** A major chord is often just notated with the name of the root and nothing else. For example a **C Major** chord will often just be written as **C**.

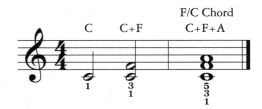

When playing the F/C chord with the left hand, the 5th finger can stay on the C while you play the other two notes with the 2nd and 1st fingers.

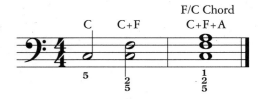

Chord Warm-ups for the Left Hand

Play the following chord warm-ups for the left hand to prepare for the songs coming up. Play slowly at first and pick up speed as you get comfortable with the notes. The letters above the music are called *chord symbols* and tell you the chords to be played. Chord symbols are commonly found in sheet music.

Track 24

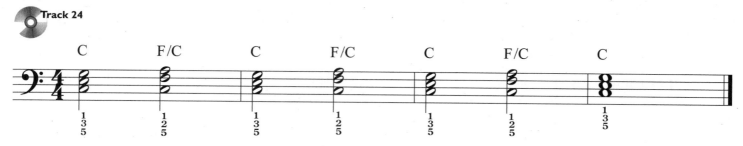

This next warm-up is similar to the previous one except the note values are now faster. You'll be playing quarter notes instead of half notes.

Track 25

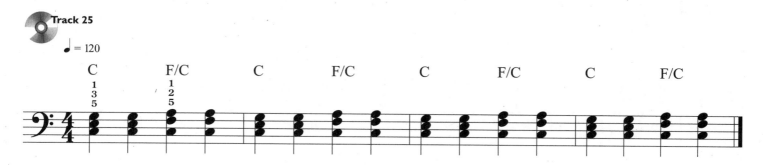

Now, let's play "Rockin' Away Again," which is "Rockin' Away" from page 20 with full chords in the left hand.

Rockin' Away Again

Track 26

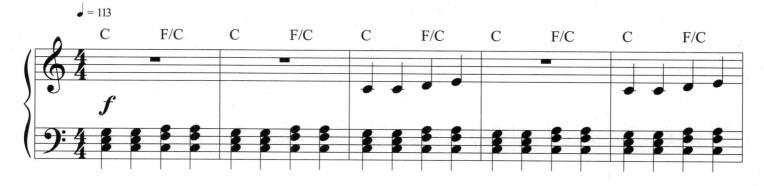

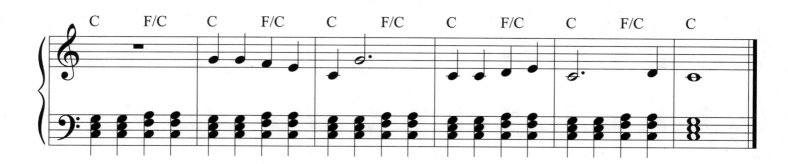

INTRODUCING THE G7 CHORD IN THE LEFT HAND

Another important rock keyboard chord is *G7*, which is part of the *dominant 7th* family of chords. Like other dominant 7th chords, G7 has four notes (G7 = G–B–D–F), but here we will drop the D, and play essentially the same chord with just three notes. This will make it easy to move to G7 from our C Major chord. Also notice that, like the F/C chord, the lowest note is not the root (G) but is B, instead, so the full name of this chord is G7/B.

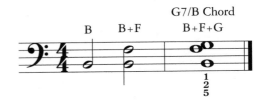

Let's try out switching between C Major and G7 chords in the left hand.

Track 27

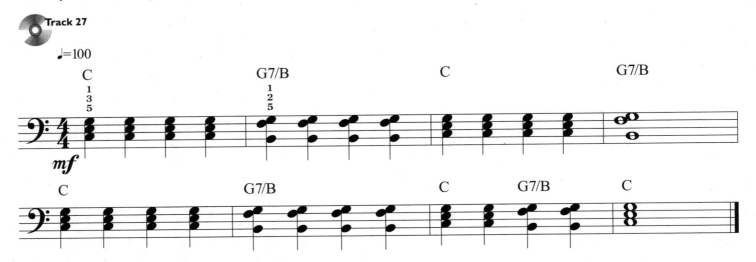

"Working" is an easy song that features C Major and G7 chords. Sing along as you play it.

Working

Track 28

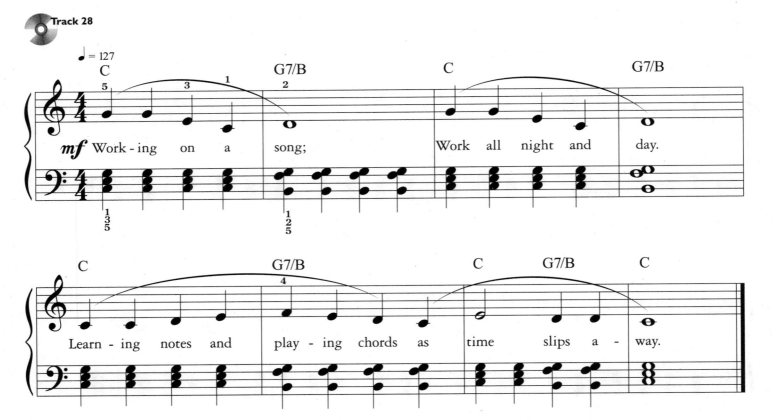

The next song is based on the popular early American tune "Oh Susannah." Here we play it in a 1950s rock style. Your left hand needs to keep a strong and steady tempo so you don't slow down.

Before playing "Susannah Rocks," warm up your left hand by playing the examples on page 23 several times. Practice until you can play them with your eyes closed!

"Susannah Rocks" includes the note A in the right hand. To play it, move your right-hand 4th finger one key to the right. This will set you up to play the A with your 5th finger. Changing fingers like this is called a *substitution*.

Susannah Rocks

Track 29

Play this song with a steady left hand, and make sure the beat is solid. Practice the first four measures first, which feature the left hand, then practice the right hand by itself. When you are comfortable with both parts, play the full song.

Memphis Calling   Track 30

Here's a simple rock song. It features a harmonized melody in the right hand.
The right hand is in *E position,* which means to put finger 1 on E. Have fun!

Come On, Move It Track 31

IMPORTANT ROOT CHORDS IN THE KEY OF C

Now that we've played a few simple melodies, let's look deeper into chords. Many rock keyboard parts rely on three-note chords called *triads*.

The *root* of a chord or triad is the note on which the chord is built. Rock music often features chords in *root position,* meaning the root note is the lowest note played. To play rock music with these chords, you will need to make large position shifts with your hands. The 1st finger of the right hand and the 5th finger of the left hand, which usually play the root notes, may need to shift three or more notes in order to switch between different chords in a sequence. These chord jumps are necessary because, unlike jazz or classical music where the lowest note of a chord is not always the root, rock music is often root dependent. Jumping around a particular key with root-position chords is one way to get that effect.

Make sure to look closely at where you are moving your fingers so that you don't miss notes when you shift to the next chord.

Since C is an important anchor note for much of beginning keyboard, let's review the C Major chord and learn its close relatives, the F Major and G Major chords.

You already know the C Major chord in root position. Let's review it below.

C Chord in the Right Hand

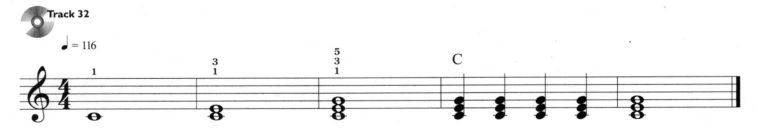

C Chord in the Left Hand

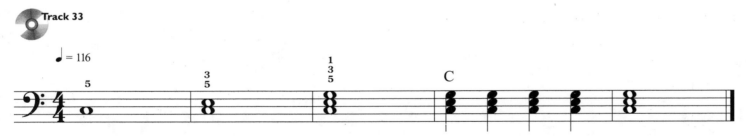

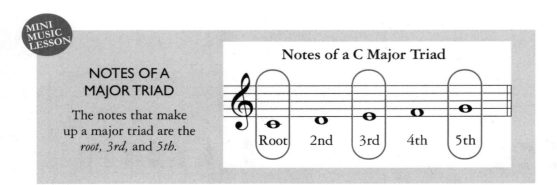

MINI MUSIC LESSON

NOTES OF A MAJOR TRIAD

The notes that make up a major triad are the *root, 3rd,* and *5th.*

Notes of a C Major Triad

Root | 2nd | 3rd | 4th | 5th

Your right-hand fingerings for a triad will correspond to the note it is playing: finger 1 plays the root, finger 3 plays the 3rd, and finger 5 plays the 5th. The left-hand fingering is just the opposite with finger 5 on the root, finger 3 on the 3rd, and finger 1 playing the 5th.

F Chord in the Right Hand

The root position of an F Major chord is made of the three notes, F, A, and C. You have played the F Major chord before, but here it is in root position.

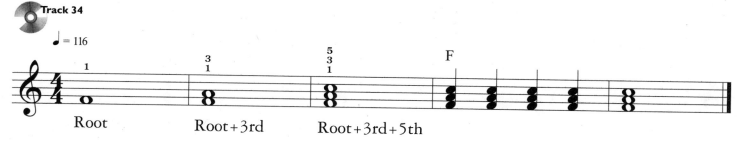

F Chord in the Left Hand

When playing the F Major chord in the left hand, watch out for the ledger line above the bass staff. It is the C note on middle C.

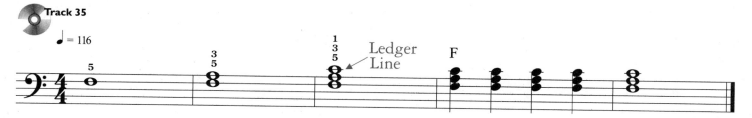

G Chord in the Right Hand

This is a simple root-position G Major chord played in the right hand.

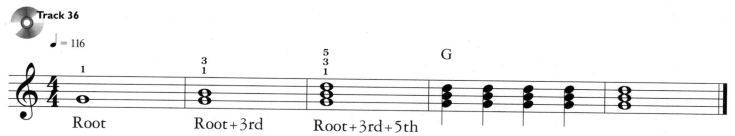

G Chord in the Left Hand

Note the ledger line above the bass staff here. This line represents middle C, so for the G Major chord below, we will be playing the note above it, which is D.

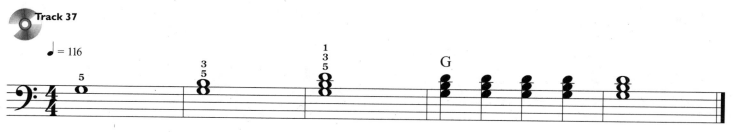

PLAYING ROOT-POSITION CHORDS IN BOTH HANDS

Let's work on playing root-position chords in both hands. In the following exercise, you will first play right-hand chords, then left-hand chords, then both hands together. To play this style of chording, often called *block chords*, you will need to make position shifts. In your right hand, play the first chord, then lift your hand and shift your 1–3–5 fingering to the next position. In the left hand, you'll be shifting your 5–3–1 fingering.

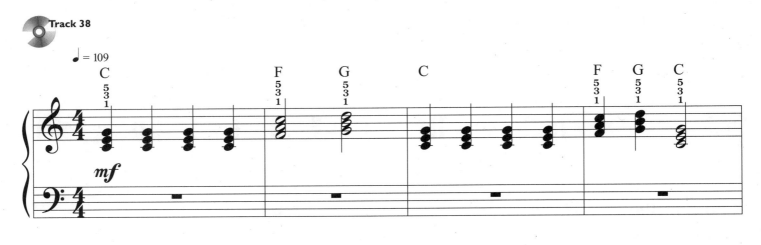

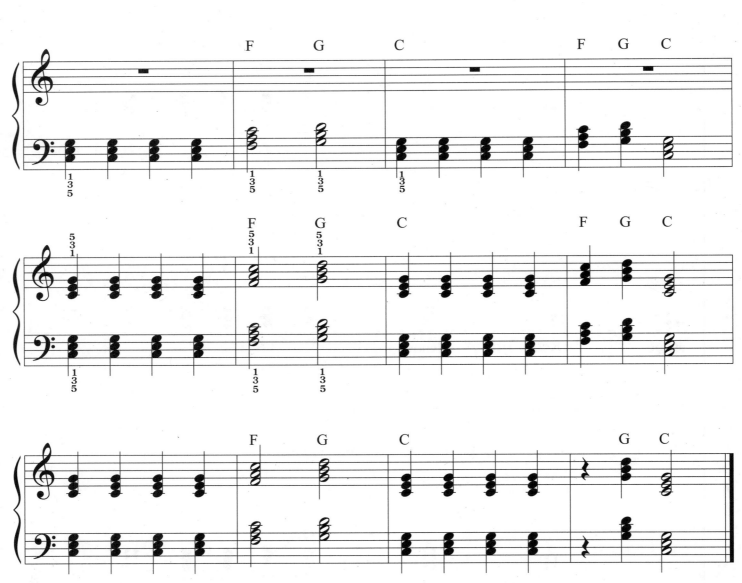

When you play chord sequences, often called *chord progressions,* it is common to only play single notes in the left hand. Following is the same chord progression from the previous page, but this version features the right hand playing chords, while the left hand plays only single root notes starting at measure 9. This produces a clearer, more balanced sound.

Track 39

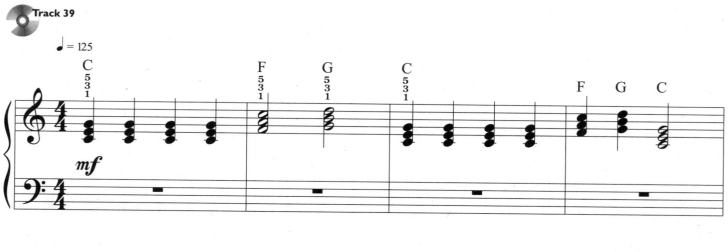

SONG WITH ROOT-POSITION C, F, AND G CHORDS

"Flying Higher" is a simple three-chord rock song. Practice the left hand alone slowly at first until the shift from C to F is smooth. Except for the last chord, the right hand is in E position throughout with finger 1 on E.

MINI MUSIC LESSON

REPEAT SIGN
At the bottom of the page, a *repeat sign* :| is used. A repeat sign means to go back to the beginning and play the piece again to the end.

Flying Higher

 Track 40

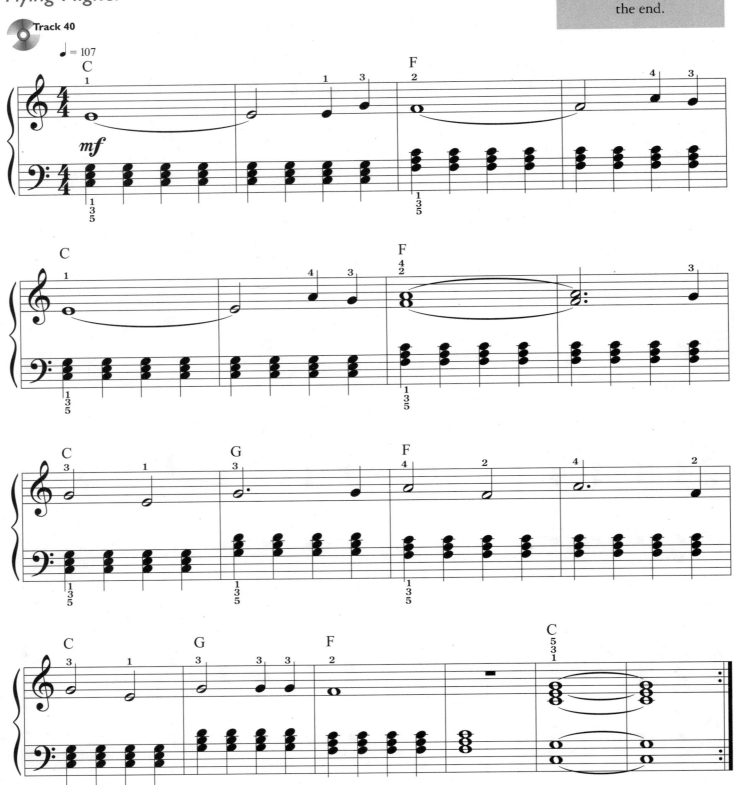

THE C MAJOR SCALE

Scales are essential tools for making all kinds of music. The C Major scale is all the white keys from one C to the next higher C note. Here is a C Major scale in the treble staff.

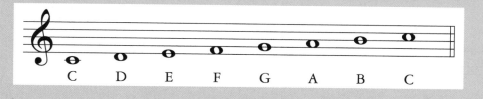

DIATONIC TRIADS AND CHORDS

Diatonic is a fancy name for chords and notes "in the scale." We can build different types of chords on each step of the C Major scale to get a wide range of colors. There are three types of chords built on the major scale:

major, minor, and diminished. Each has a different sound. The chord built on the note C is C Major. The second and third notes of the scale produce D Minor (Dmin) and E Minor (Emin) chords. On the 4th and 5th, we have

F Major and G Major chords. The 6th is an A Minor chord, and the 7th is a *diminished chord,* the B Diminished (Bdim). It's good to know about the diminished chord, but you won't need it for the songs in this book.

Here are the diatonic chords in C:

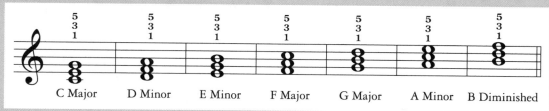

This reggae-style song features just two chords, C Major and D Minor. Play it with a light and airy feel. Notice that there is a repeat

sign facing the other way ‖: in this example. Play from the beginning as normal, but when you get to the repeat sign in the second line of

music, go back to the first repeat sign, then play to the end without repeating a second time.

Seaside Dreaming Track 41

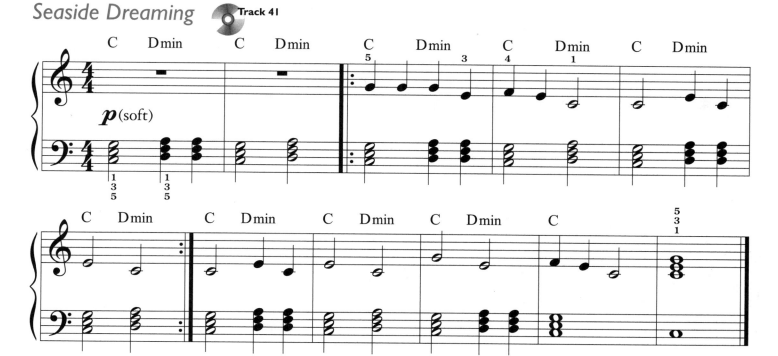

"Lost in a Dream" uses six diatonic chords—C Major, D Minor, E Minor, F Major, G Major, and A Minor— from the key of C Major. Practice playing the chords in the left hand as whole-note block chords first, then play in rhythm with the melody. Watch your right-hand position shifts.

Lost in a Dream Track 42

This song features more diatonic chords, from C Major up to A Minor.

Confidence in the Chords

Track 43

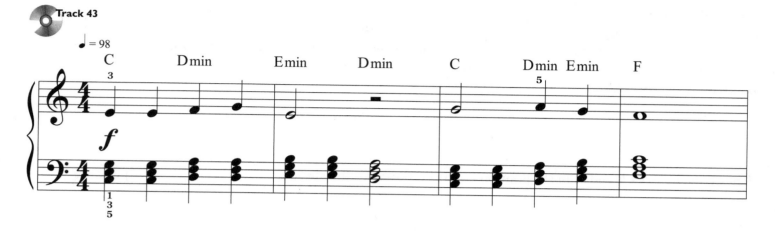

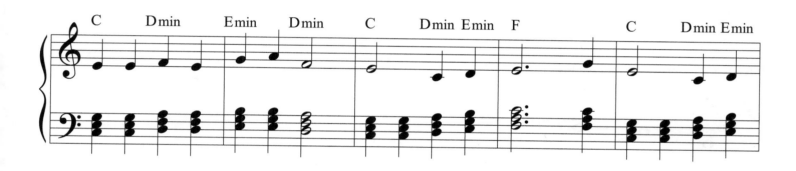

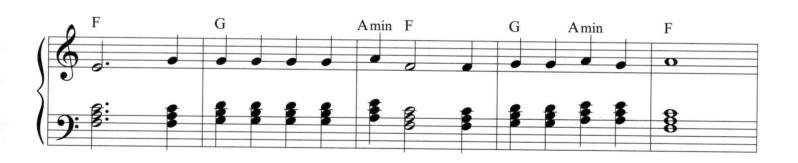

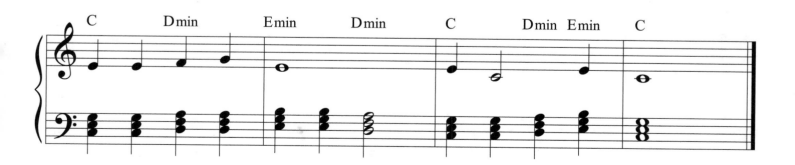

NEW HAND POSITIONS

So far, we have stayed in positions near the middle of the keyboard, but the piano, and most electronic keyboards, have many high and low keys to play. Let's explore some of these notes to extend our range of sounds on the keyboard.

The music below and on the next page uses lower notes on the keyboard. An *octave* is eight notes either higher or lower than the starting note and is the same letter name as the starting note. So, if you play middle C followed by the next C lower on the keyboard, you are playing the C one octave lower. In music notation, an octave is written either line to space, or space to line.

Here are the notes C, F, and G in the position on the keyboard you are already familiar with.

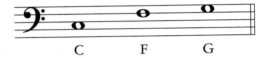

Here are C, F, and G one octave lower.

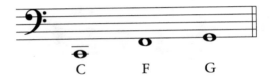

This next example is the lower D in the left hand.

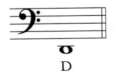

Try this warm-up for your left hand before playing "Mexican Dance Party" on the next page.

Track 44

$\quad = 223$

LA BAMBA-STYLE ROCK

"Mexican Dance Party" is a three-chord song in the style of Ritchie Valens' hit "La Bamba." The main chord progression was also used in "Twist and Shout" recorded by The Beatles, "Do You Love Me" by The Contours, and many more songs. "La Bamba" was originally a Mexican folk song.

Mexican Dance Party   Track 45

INTRODUCING THE EIGHTH NOTE AND EIGHTH REST

Eighth Note

Eighth notes are an important rhythm to learn, as they appear in all styles of music. Eighth notes are one half the value of a quarter note. So, there are two eighth notes for every quarter note. They look like quarter notes but with a *flag* added.

The eighth notes above include flags, but two or more consecutive eighth notes can also be written with a *beam*. Take a look to the right.

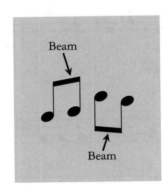

Counting Eighth Notes

Let's count eighth notes to get more familiar with them. Since we know two eighth notes make up a quarter note and one quarter note equals one beat, we will count "1 &" for every pair of eighth notes—which is equivalent to one quarter note. See the music example below.

Count out loud as you tap the beats on a table.

Count: 1   2   3   4   1 & 2 & 3 & 4 &   1   2   3 & 4   1 & 2   3   4 &   1 & 2   3 & 4

Eighth Rest

The *eighth rest* is the silent version of the eighth note. They are useful when you want short breaks in the music.

EIGHTH REST

Review of Note and Rest Values

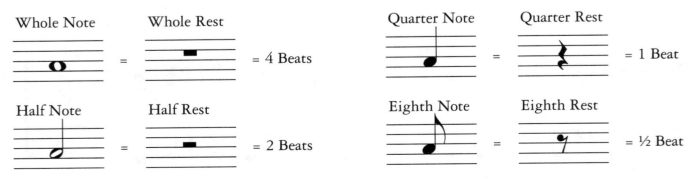

Whole Note   Whole Rest   = 4 Beats   Quarter Note   Quarter Rest   = 1 Beat

Half Note   Half Rest   = 2 Beats   Eighth Note   Eighth Rest   = ½ Beat

Here is a 1950s-style rock 'n' roll song that uses root-position chords and eighth notes. Notice that in the third line, second measure, finger 2 substitutes for finger 3 on the note F. Have fun and make it rock!

Stomping at the Drive-In   Track 46

INTRODUCING THE ARPEGGIO

An *arpeggio* is a chord played with the notes in sequence, one after the other, rather than playing them simultaneously. It gives a feeling of motion, as opposed to the stagnant feel that playing block chords might produce.

Following are some examples with arpeggios. Notice how the fingering changes between three-note and four-note arpeggios.

You can play an arpeggio on any chord. Try this arpeggio on a C Major chord.

Now play an arpeggio on a G Major chord. Keep the tempo steady.

This example incorporates a few of the diatonic chords in C Major.

Van Go Arpeggios

Track 49

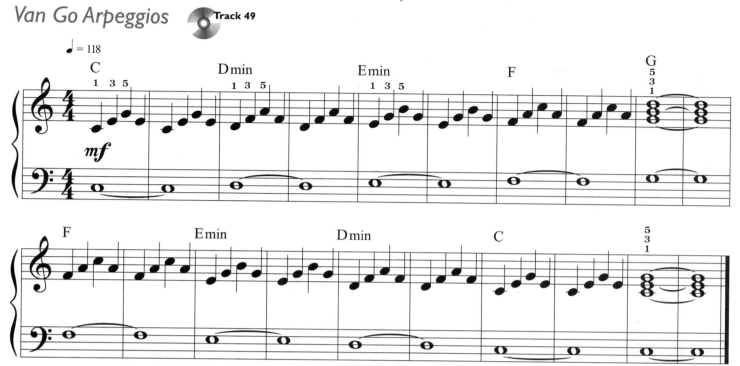

"Southland Song" is in $\frac{3}{4}$ time. Instead of four beats, which is the count in $\frac{4}{4}$ time, there are three beats in a measure. Count 1–2–3, 1–2–3 with an accent on beat 1.

Southland Song

Track 50

SONGS WITH STRONG BASSLINES

Now, play "Five Alarm Fire," which features single notes played by the left hand. We call this a *bassline.* Count the eighth notes carefully.

Five Alarm Fire   Track 51

* *Intro*, *Verse*, *Chorus*, *Break*, and other terms like this refer to different sections in a song. Each section usually sounds different from another, and some repeat like the *chorus* in this song.

SHARPS, FLATS, AND NATURALS—THE BLACK KEYS

So far you have been playing only white keys. But what about the black keys?

The black keys take their names from their neighboring white keys. They can be either *sharps* or *flats,* depending on the situation. For example, when we play the **black key to the right of middle C**, it's the note C♯ which is said *C-sharp.* If we play the black key to the left of D (in reality the exact same black key) it will be labeled D♭ or *D flat.*

SHARP

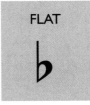

FLAT

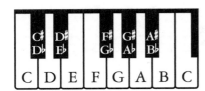

Here's a breakdown of the names of the black keys:

1. The black key to the right of C is C♯ (or its alternate name D♭)

2. The black key to the right of D is D♯ (or its alternate name E♭)

3. The black key to the right of F is F♯ (or its alternate name G♭)

4. The black key to the right of G is G♯ (or its alternate name A♭)

5. The black key to the right of A is A♯ (or its alternate name B♭)

If you wanna rock, you must throw in some sharps and flats to spice up the mix!

So far all the tunes we've learned have been in the *key of C.* This means that all the notes are white notes and the primary note of the tune is C. However, a song can be in the major key of another note other than C. Sharps or flats would be necessary to establish that other key. But more on this later.

MORE ABOUT SHARPS, FLATS, AND NATURALS

If a sharp or a flat is in a piece of music and you want to cancel that alteration (shift it back to a white key), you can use a symbol called a *natural* (♮). Sharps, flats, and naturals are also known as *accidentals.*

NATURAL

Here an A♭ is changed back to an A natural.

"House of the Rising Sun" (p.46) is in the key of *A Minor*, a *relative key* to the key C Major. An A Minor scale is a relative of the C Major scale because it also only uses the white notes. Unlike C Major, A Minor starts on A. Sometimes sharp or flat notes are added to minor scales to make them more interesting.

Even though "House of the Rising Sun" is in A Minor, it uses G♯s and F♯s in chords such as E Major and D Major. Also notice the F♮ on the F chord. This is used to remind you that the F chord is not played with an F♯ which was used in the previous measure.

Here is the D chord and the E chord used in "House of the Rising Sun."

D Major Chord

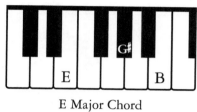

E Major Chord

HALF STEPS & WHOLE STEPS

Half Steps

A *half step* is the distance from any key to the very next key above or below (black or white).

Half Steps • No Key Between

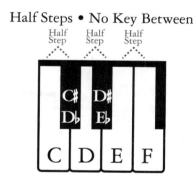

Whole Steps

A *whole step* is equal to 2 half steps. Skip one key (black or white).

Whole Steps • One Key Between

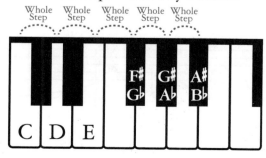

This is a song in the key of A Minor that uses arpeggios. Here is a warm up of chords you will use.

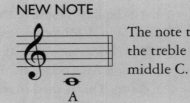

NEW NOTE

The note two ledger lines below the treble staff is the A below middle C.

Track 52

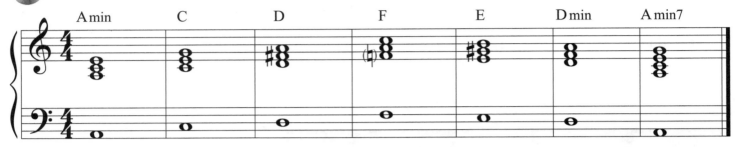

House of the Rising Sun

Track 53

♩ = 86 Intro

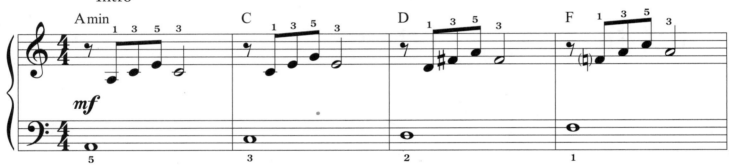

NEW DYNAMICS

mp (*mezzo piano*) = moderately soft

pp (*pianissimo*) = very soft

ppp (*pianisissimo*) = extremely soft

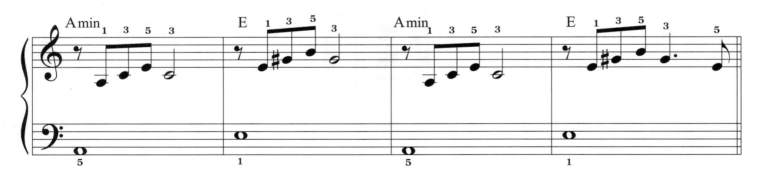

Verse

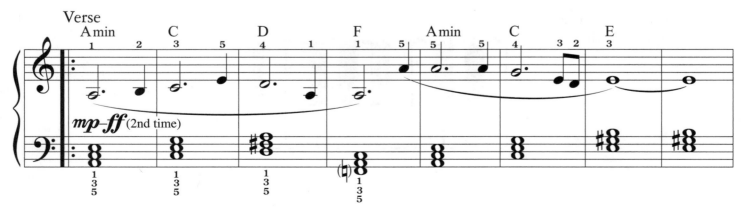

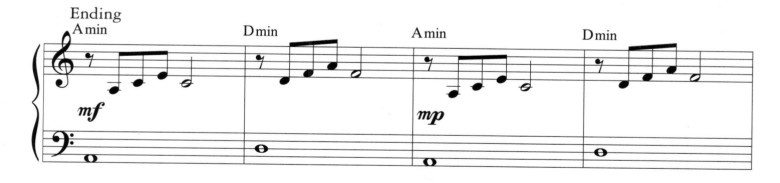

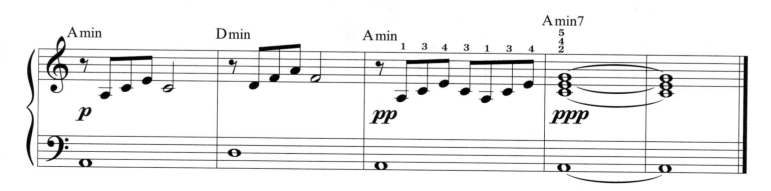

THE MAJOR CHORD AND THE MINOR CHORD
Unlocking the Mysteries of Major and Minor Chords

Major and minor chords are the most common chords in music. The major chord is often designated at the "happy" chord and the minor chord is often designated at the "sad" or "somber" chord. They are both essential to playing just about any kind of music.

Let's look at how to build a minor chord from a major chord. The formula for a major chord is root, major 3rd, and 5th. The root is the note the chord is based on. For example a C Major chord's root is the note C. The major 3rd is two whole steps or four half steps above the root. The 5th is one and a half whole steps or three half steps above the major 3rd.

Here is C Major.

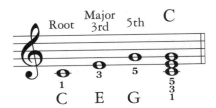

To convert the major into a minor, we take the middle note of the triad and move it down one half step, or the very next key to the left. This means the minor 3rd is only one and a half whole steps above the root, and the 5th is two whole steps above the minor 3rd.

Here is a C Minor.

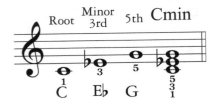

Here is a diagram of what the two chords look like on a keyboard. Practice moving the middle note of a C Major triad down to the E♭ to make the minor chord. Do it ten times, or until it feels natural to your hand.

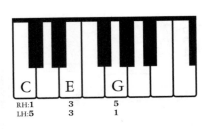

C Major Chord   C Minor Chord

This song introduces a fast change from a C Major chord to a C Minor chord and back to C Major. It is adapted from Richard Strauss's tone poem *Also sprach Zarathustra*, which was used as the opening theme from the movie *2001: A Space Odyssey*.

Space Oddity 101

Track 54

INTRODUCING OCTAVES

Octaves are important in your keyboard playing. Finger octaves 1–5 for white keys and 1–4 for black keys. Keep your hands in position as you move your arm up and down the keyboard. Practice these octave scales slowly until your hands feel comfortable with this technique.

NOTE: Ledger lines can be confusing to even experienced music readers. When in doubt, count the ledger lines to identify the proper notes and mark them with a pencil.

Play this example with just your right hand.

Track 55

Here is the same exercise for the left hand.

Track 56

After you feel comfortable with the above exercises, put both hands together as in the example below.

Track 57

"Yo-Yo Heave Ho," on the next page, uses octaves to make the melody sound stronger and more powerful.

PLAYING OCTAVE MELODIES IN THE RIGHT HAND AND LEFT HAND

Yo-Yo Heave Ho (Volga Boatman Song)

Track 58

NEW NOTE

The note three ledger lines below the bass staff is A.

ALTERNATING OCTAVES FOR QUICK AND EASY ACCOMPANIMENT

A common technique for playing rock piano is *rocking octaves* in the left hand. Here are some exercises for both hands using rocking octaves. Finger the octaves as if you were going to play them simultaneously, but rock your hand so the notes are played separately.

This next tune is a rock arrangement of a well-known American Revolutionary War song. For the chorus section, the left hand plays a pumping, alternating octave part.

NOTE: The first four measures on the recording for this song are a drum introduction. The big **4** over the solid black line at the beginning means the piano player rests (doesn't play) for a full four measures, or if you're counting, a full 16 beats (count **1**–2–3–4, **2**–2–3–4, **3**–2–3–4, **4**–2–3–4).

Rocking Yankee Doodle

Track 60

♩ = 165

PLAYING WITH THE LEFT HAND IN THE TREBLE CLEF AND PLAYING WITH THE RIGHT HAND IN THE BASS CLEF

The grand staff can be changed to make reading the music easier when the music is in ranges that extend outside the standard grand staff. The right hand can sometimes be written in bass clef, and the left hand can sometimes be in the treble clef.

If a composer wants to stack a lot of high notes, they may use a treble clef in the left hand. Similarly, if the music is mostly low notes, the right hand could be in the bass clef.

Play the following exercise with the *right hand*. Be sure to use the designated fingering.

In the next example, finger 3 must *cross over* the thumb (finger 1) to play the sixth note of the scale. This technique is essential in keyboard music to make playing scale-like passages sound smooth.

It is important to avoid twisting the hand when crossing over.

Be aware that when going down the scale, the finger goes over the thumb, but the reverse is true when going up the scale: the thumb crosses under the fingers.

Right Hand

Track 61

Here is a similar exercise for the *left hand* in the treble clef. Follow the designated fingering. Here, when going up the scale, finger 3 crosses over the thumb.

Left Hand

Track 62

Here's an easy, bluesy song. It could be played with just two fingers, but you should use all five to make the playing smooth. Notice that the right hand is notated in the bass clef. The second

half of the song is the same as the first, except down one octave to get a deeper rock sound.

Be sure you play the designated B♭ starting in measure 4. Remember, an

accidental lasts for the rest of the bar. Also, the note E♭ is used in the right hand on the 2nd ledger line starting with measure 8.

The Two-Finger Blues

Track 63

♩ = 143

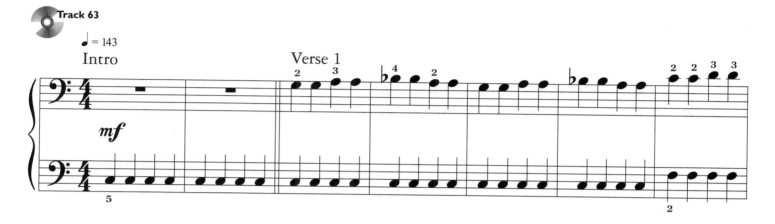

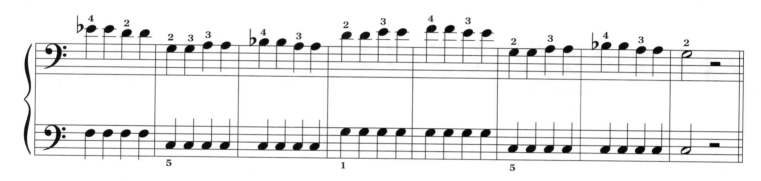

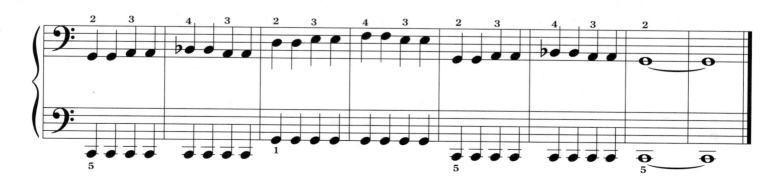

PREPARATION FOR "WHEN THE SAINTS ROCK"

In "When the Saints Rock" on the next page, the left hand plays a boogie
figure that alternates between the 5th and 6th of each chord, similar to the
one on page 20. Reviewing those riffs will help you master this new pattern.
It is faster and uses eighth notes as well as quarter notes. Play the following
warm-ups with a steady, strong pulse.

Play this exercise until the shift from the index finger to the thumb is smooth and strong.

Here is a similar exercise but with a lively eighth-note rhythm. Repeat it several times.

Count: 1   2   3 & 4 (&)

The next exercise uses the above rhythms but shifts up and down the keyboard to play the chord progression.

Track 64

When the Saints Rock

Track 65

MINI MUSIC LESSON

ACCENT

Play this note a little louder

SWING FEEL AND ALTERNATING OCTAVES

This next song is played with a *swing feel* (or *shuffle feel*). Eighth notes are usually played evenly, dividing the beat in half. When playing rhythms in swing feel, the two eighth notes are played unevenly, with the first eighth note held longer than the second. The rhythm for eighth notes is *long–short*, *long–short*, etc. Listen to the recording to hear how it sounds. It gives the rhythm a skipping, jazzy feel! Play swing eighths whenever you see "Swing 8ths" or "Shuffle feel" at the beginning of a tune.

This song also uses the rocking octave pattern discussed on page 52. However, it will sound different now because of swing eighths.

Hot Time Shuffle

ROCK BALLAD STYLE

Here is a song that is in the style of the great classic-rock ballads. These four chords (C, G, A Minor and F) are used in many popular songs. The chords are easy to play, so be sure you bring out the melody, and, even though there are no words, play it with feeling and make it sing!

Rainy Day Sunshine Track 67

CHORD INVERSIONS

So far in this book, most of the chords we've played are in root position (page 28). However, sometimes a chord is played with a note other than the root in the bass (see page 22). For example, instead of playing a C chord with a C as the lowest note of the chord, we can move the bass note to an E (*1st inversion*) or a G (*2nd inversion*). See the examples below.

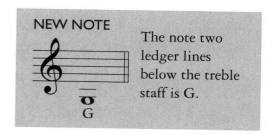

NEW NOTE The note two ledger lines below the treble staff is G.

Here is a C chord in root, 1st, and 2nd inversions.

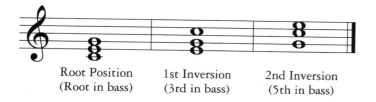

Root Position (Root in bass)   1st Inversion (3rd in bass)   2nd Inversion (5th in bass)

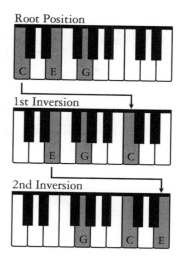

Here is a G chord in root, 1st, and 2nd inversions.

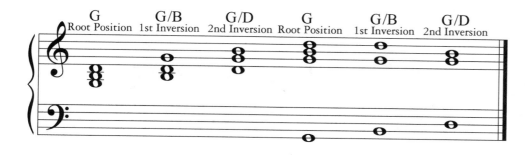

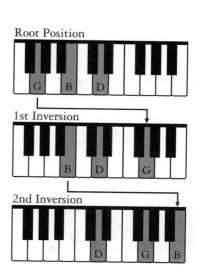

C/E = First Inversion C

C/G = Second Inversion C

CHORD INVERSIONS IN ROCK

Play these right- and left-hand figures. The slash chords are the inverted
chords. Play with a "swing feel" (page 58).

Body Rocking Baby

Track 68

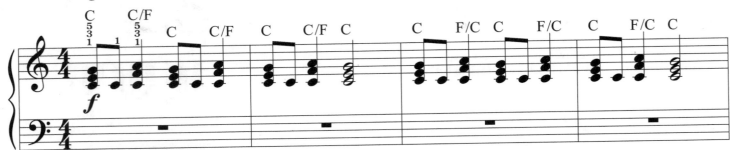

Often the backbone of 1950s rock piano was the constant eighth-note chords while the left hand played long held root notes. Sometimes,

when a full band plays along, the left hand is omitted to let the bass guitar and rhythm guitar fill in the lower parts, but, in this example,

play roots in the left hand to solidify the harmonic structure.

Friday Night Dance Party

 Track 69

KEY SIGNATURES AND MORE SCALES

The *key signature* is a group of sharps or flats shown at the beginning of the staff that indicates which notes are sharp or flat throughout the entire piece. When you use a key signature, you don't need to write an accidental in front of every black key.

For example when playing in the *key of G*, every F is sharp. In the *key of D*, every F and C is sharp. In the *key of A*, every F, C, and G is sharp.

When a key signature is used, it is put at the beginning of every staff, right after the clef. See the diagram below.

We can also use flats to signify key signatures. In the *key of F* every B is flat. In the *key of B♭* every B and E is FLAT.

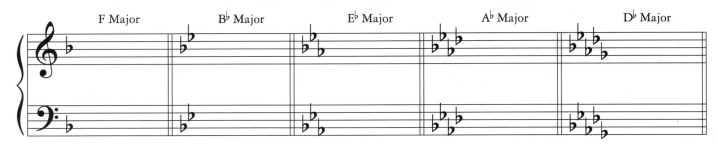

Here are some easy major scales written in different keys. Familiarize yourself with the sharps and flats.

Track 70

MAJOR 7TH AND DOMINANT 7TH CHORDS

So far in this book we have played songs based on *triads*—three-note chords like a major or minor chord. What happens if we take a triad, and add an extra note and make it a four note chord? This greatly expands the harmonic possibilities available to us.

As you have learned, major and minor chords are made by stacking three notes at intervals of a 3rd. If we add another note on top of that triad (again, a 3rd away) we get a *7th chord*. For example, by adding a B above the G in a C Major chord it becomes a 7th chord.

Here are two different C 7th chords: the *major 7th* (Cmaj7) and the *dominant 7th* (C7). The major 7th chord is made by adding a note a major 3rd (four half steps) above the G (B♮). The dominant 7th chord is made by adding a note a minor 3rd (three half steps) above the G (B♭).

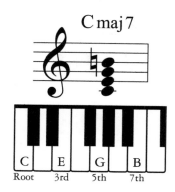 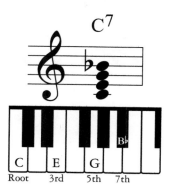

Play both of the above chords and listen to the difference. The major seventh is a sweet, somewhat dreamy-sounding chord. It's often been called the chord of "love songs".

The dominant 7th is harsher sounding, and it's a great chord for rock music.

Below are three dominant 7th chords. The dominant 7th chord is so common that it's usually written with just a "7" with no "maj" or "min" designation.

Play the following three chords, and make up your own dominant 7ths with the other triads you know.

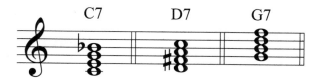

USING DOMINANT 7TH CHORDS WITH INVERSIONS

One of the classic riffs of rock and jazz is the root chord (in this next example, the C) moving to the 2nd inversion chord on the 4th step of the scale (in this next example, the F/C chord) followed by the root chord with a dominant 7th and then back. This riff has been used in many songs, for example the Doors' "When the Music's Over" and the jazz standard "Watermelon Man."

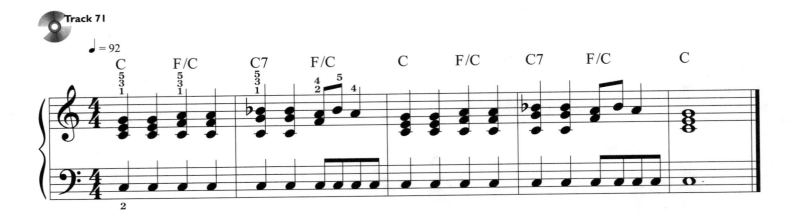

Practice this pattern below to become familiar with the same riff in the key of G.

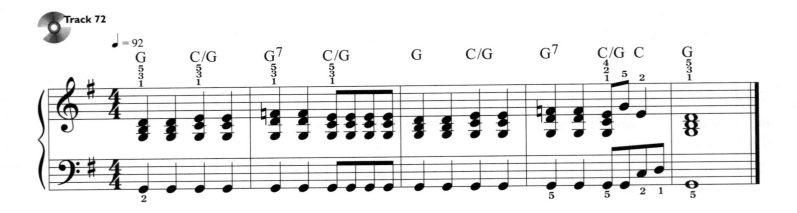

"Where's Louie?" (page 68) is in the key of G. The key of G has one sharp, F♯. However, the song makes extensive use of the G7 chord which includes an F♮ so that every F has a natural sign in front of it. This use of a dominant 7th chord on the root of the key gives the song a bluesy feel.

WARM UP FOR "WHERE'S LOUIE?"

Here are some exercises to get your chops up for "Where's Louie?".
Practice these separately before playing "Where's Louie?".

First, practice the right hand for the intro and chorus sections. Practice this
5–6 times.

Now, add the left hand to the above rhythm. Be sure you play this with a
steady beat. Practice slowly with a metronome and count out the rhythm
until this feels great!

The verse section has a different feel. Try this exercise. Count out the beats
slowly at first.

Here is a tune in the style of "Louie Louie" by Richard Berry (and made famous by the Kingsmen). This rock standard is one of the most important early "garage band" classics.

Where's Louie?

MINI MUSIC LESSON

GRACE NOTE

Very short note played immediately before the next beat

SYNCOPATION—GOTTA HAVE THAT RHYTHM!

Good rhythm is the backbone of all music, but with rock music it is especially important. *Syncopation* is the shifting of accents in a line of music from strong beats to a weak beats. Notice where the strong and weak beats occur in the following example.

Syncopation also applies to faster rhythms.

Here's a syncopation example with eighth notes. Count the beats out loud.

Track 77

Below is a comparison of rhythms with and without syncopation. Notice that the notes that land on beat 4 of measure 1 and beat 1 of measure 2 in the conventional example are moved over one eighth note to create displaced accents in the syncopated example.

Conventional

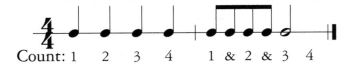

Syncopated

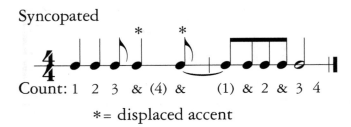

*= displaced accent

MORE SYNCOPATION

The first bar of the next example uses more syncopation. Count the beats and notice the off-beat hit on the & of beat 2 as you play.

Track 78

Here is a warm up for the next song. The right hand starts out just like the previous example but with an added part for the left hand. Keep the rhythm steady and lively. Count out loud. Practice this for several minutes before attempting "Down Home Feeling" on page 72.

Track 79

Down Home Feeling

"The Piano Guy" is in the style of Billy Joel's "Piano Man." This is another song in $\frac{3}{4}$ time, also known as *waltz time*. Count 1–2–3, 1–2–3 with a slight accent on the first beat of each measure.

The Piano Guy

Track 81

♩ = 133

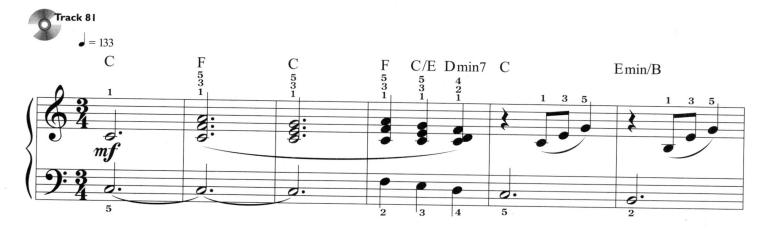

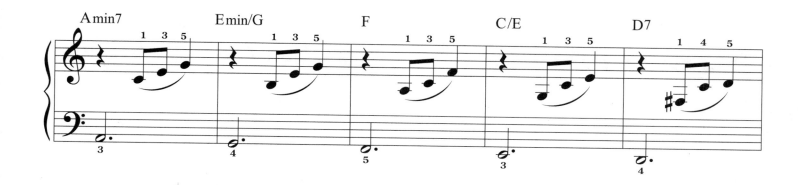

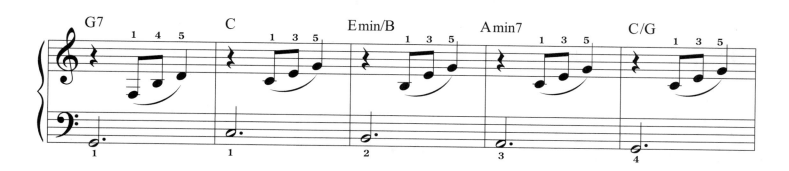

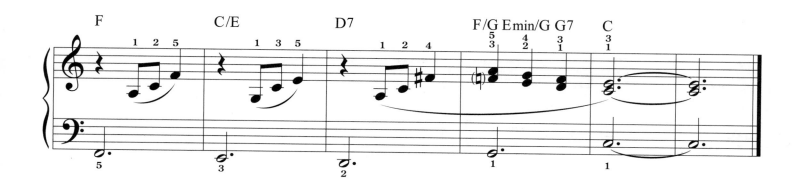

The next tune is in the style of piano pop songs like "Clocks" by Coldplay.
You can play the left hand one octave lower for a deeper sound.

Timepieces Track 82

MORE LEFT-HAND ROCK AND ROLL PATTERNS

Here are a few more left-hand rock patterns for piano. They can really kick a song up a notch, and put the rock in the roll!

The rhythms in these exercises are simpler than those you've been playing, but they require good hand strength and steadiness to make them work. Use a metronome with a moderate tempo and keep a steady beat as you practice.

Left Hand No. 1

Track 83

Left Hand No. 2

Track 84

Swing feel

TRIPLETS

The song on the next page uses a new rhythm called a *triplet*. A triplet is a group of three notes played evenly in the time of two. In this case, there are three eighth notes in the time of two. There are several ways to count triplets, but one of the most common ways is to count each group of three as "1–and–ah, 2–and–ah, 3–and–ah, 4–and–ah." Here is an excerpt of triplets to practice for the song "The Zombieland Boogie" on page 76.

Track 85

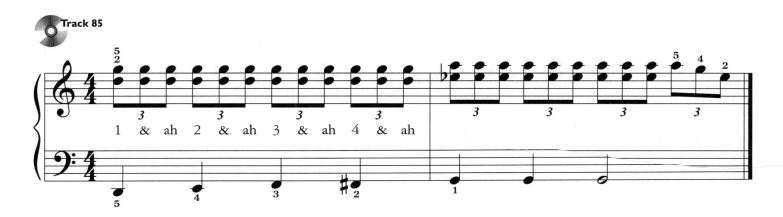

The Zombieland Boogie

Play this song with a strong left-hand rhythm. Practice one hand at a time before trying to put it all together. Count the beats to keep the rhythm steady.

ARPEGGIOS WITH SYNCOPATION

Arpeggios can be made more interesting by adding a *push*, or slight syncopation, to the figure. Here is an arpeggio played with a syncopation on the & of beat 2. Count it out and play it slowly until it feels comfortable.

Track 87

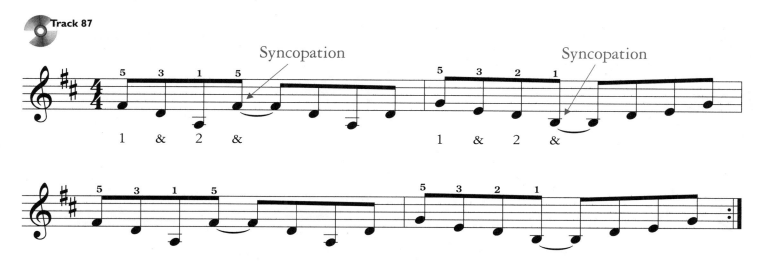

VERY LOW NOTES ON THE PIANO

You can really get an amazing sound by using the ultra low notes on the keyboard. The only difficulty is that those notes are written using multiple ledger lines. But by counting down the notes under the staff we can determine what those notes are. In this case they are a D played in octaves and a low G note. Let them ring to support the chords with bass.

Track 88

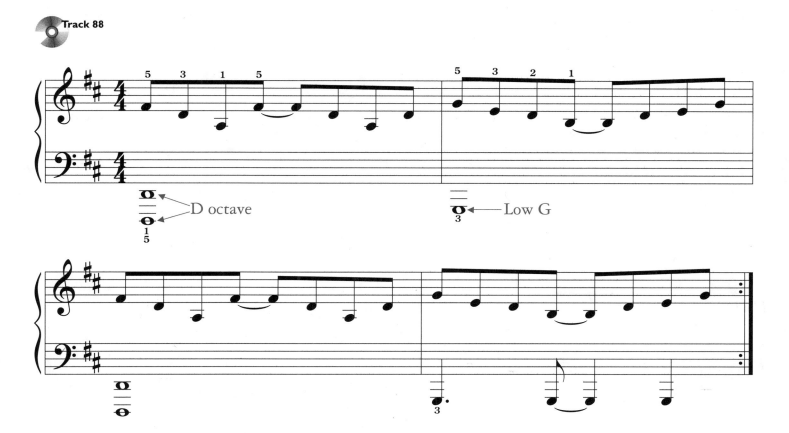

Ben Folds is one of the most popular pianists in rock. Here is a song in the style of "Brick" by Ben Folds Five.

Note that there are very low notes in the bass clef, namely the low D in measure one, and the low G in measure two. If you must, **take a pencil and mark the low notes** to help you remember their note names.

Downtown Coffee Shop   Track 89

Here is a song that is similar to the bluesy songs of the hard rocking 1970s and '80s. Sometimes the electric organ was played through a guitar amplifier with distortion to match the heavier guitar tones. Rock hard with this song!

Purple Smoke Rings

Track 90

* A "Tag" or "Coda" is an ending of the song

DICTIONARY OF ESSENTIAL CHORDS

Here is a brief list of essential major and minor chords for the right hand.

Good luck with your musical journey! For more study, see *Beginning Rock Keyboard* (18436), published by Alfred Music.